Handbook of Common
Macrame´ Knots

TABLE OF CONTENTS

FOREWORD

Because macrame' has its own lingo and its own techniques, this book was written as a guide to learning the basics. You can make marvelous projects with only one knot. And the more knots you learn, the wider variety of designs you can achieve. This is one craft where knowing a little lets you create a lot. This book is divided into three main sections. The first, and main section, includes illustrations and explanations showing and telling how to tie the various knots and knot patterns, e. g., Lark's head, square knot, clove hitch, overhand. In the second section we offer some hints which will help when macraming. And the third section is a glossary of macrame' terms.

Knots And Knot Patterns

The **LARK'S HEAD** is used as the starting knot to tie lengths of cord onto a horizontal holding cord, buckles, rings, dowels, or twigs. It is also used for decorative patterns.

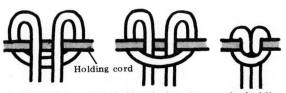

Holding cord

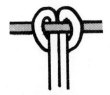

1. Fold the cord in half and place it over the holding cord. Pull the loop down behind the holding cord, and pull the two ends down and thru the loop. Pull tight.

Reverse Lark's head.

Tie 7 cords onto a holding cord with the Lark's head, see page 4 for instruction. Angle the holding cord and pin to secure shape. This makes a good beginning for a belt.

2. This Lark's head is also known as the Reverse Double Half Hitch. One knotting cord is used here to tie the series of Lark's heads. Loop the cord over and under the ring, then over itself. Next bring it under and over the ring then down and thru the loop. Pull tight.

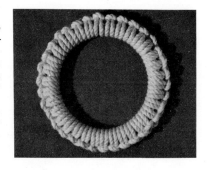

ALTERNATING LARK'S HEAD BRAID:

This braid is similiar to the No. 2 Lark's head above except two knotting cords are used here. First the far right cord is knotted around the 2 center anchor cords, then the far left cord is knotted around the center 2 cords. The braid continues the alternating left-right pattern.

5

1 2 3 4 5 6

DOUBLE ALTERNATING LARK'S HEAD BRAID: This braid is knotted using the alternating Lark's head braid, page 5; but here there are 4 knotting cords. Cords 1&6 knot around 2&5 respectively and no. 3 &4 cords cross each other and alternate knotting onto cord 2 then 5.

PICOTS *are any number of small loops forming an ornamental edge.*

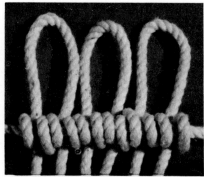

PICOT 1, CLOVE HITCH WITH LOOP: Tie the middle of a cord onto a holding cord using the clove hitch knot, see page 15 for clove hitch instructions. The left cord will hang down below the holding cord, and the right is pinned at the desired loop height, then brought back down and tied with the clove hitch to the holding cord. Each cord is mounted in this fashion.

PICOT 2, CLOVE HITCH WITH OVERHAND KNOT IN LOOP: This picot is tied the same way as Picot 1, with the added variation of tying an overhand knot at the peak of the loop. See page 21 for overhand knot instructions.

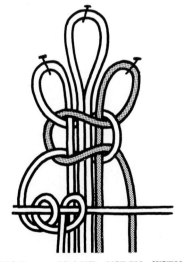

PICOT 3, CLOVE HITCH WITH THREE LOOPS JOINED BY A SQUARE KNOT: First double a cord and pin the loop to a board. Repeat with 2 other cords. There are now 6 cords. Tie a square knot using the far left and far right cord to knot around the other 4 cords. See pages 9 & 10 for square knot instruction. Next secure each cord to the holding cord using the clove hitch, see page 15 for clove hitch instructions.

Size: 4" x 7¼"

Macrame' Angel by Bobi Hall, Owner
of Bobi's Hobbys, Alhambra, California

PICOT 4, CLOVE HITCH SEMI-CIRCLE CHAIN: Attach one cord onto a holding cord using the Lark's head, see page 4 for instructions. Position the Lark's head so that the cord ends are above the holding cord. Knot cord 1 around cord 2 in a semicircle using the clove hitch, see page 15 for instructions. To attach the semicircle back onto the holding cord, knot each cord around the holding cord, using the clove hitch knot. Add the additional knotting cords with Lark's heads so that the ends fall beneath the holding cord.

The **SQUARE KNOT** *is one of the basic macrame' knots. A wide variety of patterns can be achieved with this single knot. A few of the variations follow.*

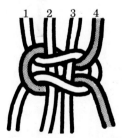

LEFT-HAND HALF KNOT: Cord 4 goes under 3 and 2 and over 1. Cord 1 goes over 2 and 3 and down thru the loop. Pull tight.

LEFT-HAND SQUARE KNOT: First tie the left-hand half knot. To tie the second half knot, cord 1 goes over 3 and 2 and under 4. Cord 4 goes under 2 and 3 and up thru the loop. Pull tight.

9

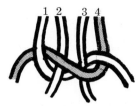

RIGHT-HAND HALF KNOT: Cord 4 goes over 3 and 2 and under 1. Cord 1 goes under 2 and 3 and up thru the loop. Pull tight.

RIGHT-HAND SQUARE KNOT: Tie the right hand half knot first. To tie the second half knot, cord 1 goes under 3 and 2 and over 4. Cord 4 goes over 2, and 3 and down thru the loop. Pull tight.

Square knot with one filler cord.

Square knot with four knotters & two fillers.

Square knot with six filler cords.

SQUARE KNOT BUTTON: Tie at least three square knots. Bring the two filler cords up over the knots and down between the filler cords at the top. Pull these cords down to form a button. Tie a square knot directly beneath the button to hold it firmly.

HALF KNOT SINNET: When the half knot (either left or right-hand) is repeatedly tied, it naturally forms a twisting design. See pages 9 & 10 for half knot instructions.

SQUARE KNOT SINNET: When the square knot is tied repeatedly, a flat pattern results.

SINNET OF ALTERNATING
FILLER CORDS:

Four cords are used in this pattern. First a square knot is tied with the left 3 cords, next a square knot is tied using the right 3 cords. The square knots here have only one center filler cord.

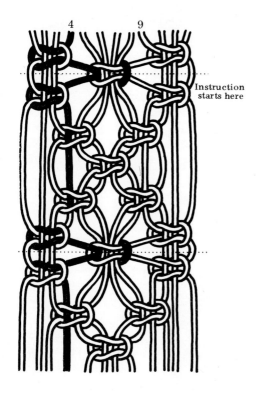

4   9

Instruction
starts here

SQUARE KNOT X PATTERN WITH MULTI-FILLER SQUARE KNOT SPACER: There are 12 cords used in this pattern of square knots, see pages 9&10 for instructions. First tie a square knot with the left 4 cords. Use the right 4 cords to tie a square knot in line with the first. In the second row, put aside the first 2 cords and tie a square knot using the next 4 cords; tie a square knot with the adjacent 4. For the third row tie only one square knot using the 4 center cords. To complete the X pattern, reverse the above process. When 5 rows are tied completing the X pattern, tie the square knot spacer using cords 4&9 to knot around the center 4 cords. Now start the X pattern again working into the center than out again.

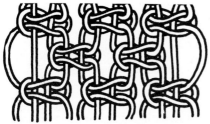

ALTERNATING SQUARE KNOT:
There are 12 cords used in this pattern of square knots, see pages 9&10 for instructions. For the first row tie a square knot with the left 4 cords. Repeat with the middle 4 cords then the right 4 cords. The second row has 2 square knots. Put aside the first 2 cords and tie a square knot with the

This photo shows alternating rows of three and four knots.

next 4, then the following 4 cords, leaving 2 cords unknotted on the right side as well. Repeat this alternating pattern of knotting 3 square knots in one row and 2 in the next.

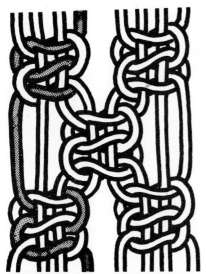

This photo shows alternating rows of three and four knots.

ALTERNATING SQUARE KNOT PLUS ONE HALF KNOT: Tie 1 square knot and 1 half knot with the left then the right 4 cords. See pages

9&10 for square knot instructions. Next tie 1 square knot plus 1 half knot with the center 4 cords. Repeat this alternating pattern.

13

SQUARE KNOT PATTERN WITH INTERCHANGING KNOTTERS & FILLERS: The square knot is used in this pattern, see pages 9&10 for instructions. The variation in this design is achieved by pulling the knotters into the filler position and the fillers into the knotting position after each square knot is tied.

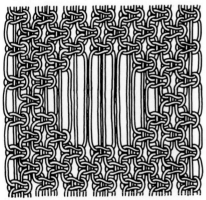

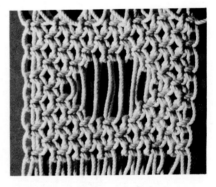

ALTERNATING SQUARE KNOTS WITH FLOATING CORDS: The alternating square knot is used in this pattern, see page 13 for instructions. The first row has 7 square knots, the second has 6 and the third has 7. In the fourth row, put aside the first 2 cords and tie a square knot with the next 4 cords, then the following 4. Leave 8 cords unknotted and tie a square knot, and then another next to it leaving 2 unknotted cords on the right side. For the fifth row, tie a square knot with the left 4 cords then the next 4. Leave 12 cords unknotted and tie one square knot then another with the 4 cords next to it. For the sixth row, put aside 2 cords and tie 1 square knot. Leave 14 unknotted cords then tie another square knot. Reverse the row instructions to finish the floating cord triangle.

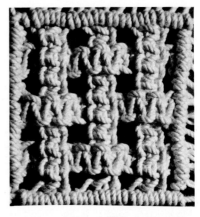

WEAVING SQUARE KNOT
SINNETS: Square knot sinnets are

woven to create a different pattern.
See page 11 for square knot sinnet.

The **CLOVE HITCH** *(also called the Double Half Hitch) can be knotted horizontally, diagonally and vertically. Many variations of the basic knot are shown on the following pages.*

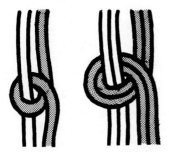

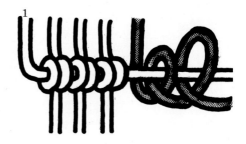

HALF HITCH: To tie the half hitch loop the right cord over then under the left cord, then over itself. The number of cords used to knot may also be varied for a different effect.

HORIZONTAL CLOVE: Cord 1, the knot-bearer, is held horizontally over the other cords. Each knotting cord cord goes around cord 1 twice, looping over then under.

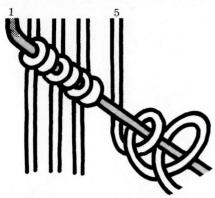

DIAGONAL CLOVE: Cord 1, the knot-bearer, is held diagonally over the other cords. Each cord goes around cord 1 twice, looping over then under. Cord 5 is shown knotting around cord 1.

VERTICAL CLOVE: In this design, there is one knotting cord, 1, and many knot-bearers, 2-4. Cord 1 loops around all the other cords twice.

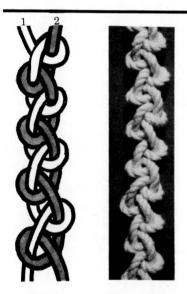

ALTERNATING HALF HITCH CHAIN: Use the half hitch to tie cord 1 around cord 2, see page 15 for half hitch instructions. Next tie a half hitch with cord 2 knotting around cord 1. Continue this alternating pattern.

SINNET OF HALF HITCHES: When the half hitch is tied repeatedly, a twisting pattern will automatically develop. See page 15 for half hitch instructions.

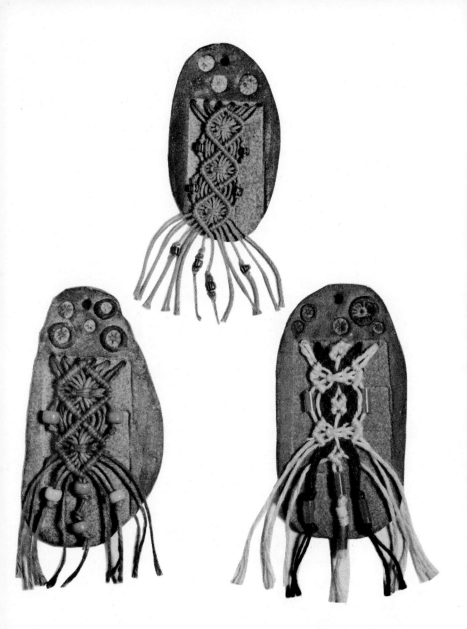

Ceramic and Macrame'
size, 3" x 5"

Dolores Schiffert, Artist
Laguna Beach, Cal.

17

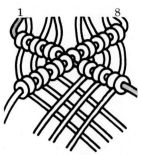

X PATTERN FORMED BY DIA-
GONAL CLOVE HITCHES: The diagonal clove is used to create this design, see page 16 for instructions.
First use cord 1 as the knot-bearer

and clove hitch cords 2-4 around it.
Next hold cord 8 in a diagonal position and knot cords 7-1 around it.
To finish the X pattern, knot cords
5-7 around 1.

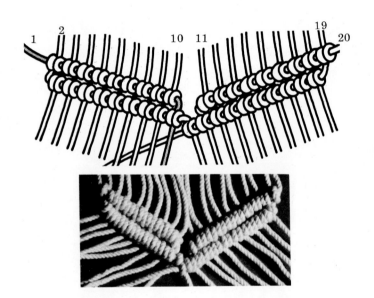

V PATTERN FORMED BY DIA-
GONAL CLOVE HITCHES: To knot
this pattern, use the diagonal clove,
see page 16. Use cord 1 as the knot-
bearer and clove hitch cords 2-10
over it, knotting from left to right.
To knot the second row, use cord 2

as the knot-bearer and clove hitch
cords 3-10 over it. Next use cord 20
as the knot-bearer and clove hitch
cords 19-11; and for the second row
use cord 19 as the knot-bearer and
clove hitch cords 18-11 and cord 2
around it.

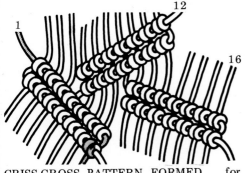

CRISS-CROSS PATTERN FORMED BY DIAGONAL CLOVE HITCHES: Sixteen cords are used here knotting with the diagonal clove, see page 16.

for instructions. First no. 12 cord is used as the knot-bearer, then 11. Next 1&2 are used, then 9 & 16.

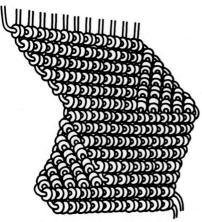

ANGLED CLOVE HITCH: Pin twelve cords to a board. Use the first cord as the knot-bearer and tie a row of horizontal clove hitches knotting from left to right, see page 15 for instructions. In the second row, use the second cord as the knot-bearer and tie another row of horizontal clove hitches. Leave the knot-bearing cords hanging on the right side. Continue by tying 4 more rows of horizontal clove hitches using the next cord as knot-bearer for each row.

Next use the first knot-bearing cord and tie a row of vertical clove hitches as shown on page 16. Use the second knot-bearing cord and tie a row of vertical clove hitches. Repeat until five rows are tied. Use the last knotter as the knot-bearer and work from right to left tying 6 horizontal clove hitch rows. Remember to use a different cord as knot-bearer for each row; this gives the angling appearance. Repeat vertical clove hitches as above.

19

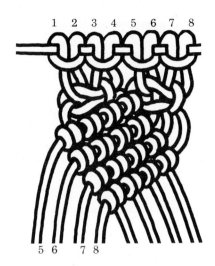

BERRY KNOT

BERRY KNOT: Mount 4 cords with Lark's head, see page 4. Tie a square knot with the left 4 cords, see pages 9&10 for instructions. Repeat with right 4 cords. First use cord 5 as the knot-bearer tying from right to left and tie diagonal clove hitches with cords 4-1. Tie 3 more rows directly beneath the first using cords 6,7&8 as knot-bearers.

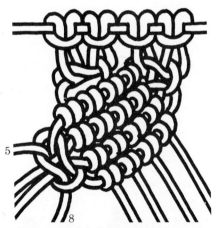

Pull cords 5-8 tight and push up the rows of diagonal cloves so the knot becomes slightly rounded. Now tie a square knot with these cords.

The **OVERHAND KNOT** *is very simple to tie and is sometimes used to start cords, or end cords so they won't fray. This knot can also be tied in several interesting patterns.*

Single cord

Two cords

Single cord and one filler

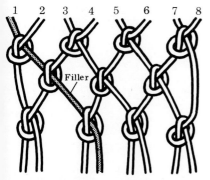

1   2   3   4   5   6   7   8

Filler

ALTERNATING OVERHAND:
Each overhand knot is tied around a filler; see above illustration. The first row has 4 overhand knots and the second has 3. To achieve this pattern, continue alternating the number of knots in each row.

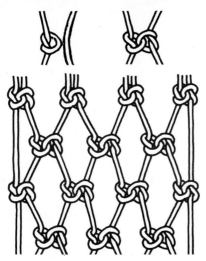

ALTERNATING INTERTWINING OVERHAND: Tie a loose overhand knot with the left cord. Then tie an overhand knot with your right cord knotting thru the loop of the first knot. Pull cords tight. Follow the Alternating Overhand pattern on pg 21.

Ornamental Knots

COIL KNOT: One end of a cord is twisted several times around the longer cord. Bring the loose end from behind, through the loop and to the front. Pull gently until a coil is formed. The more twists you make the longer the coil will be.

JOSEPHINE KNOT: Use the left 2 cords and make a loop.

Lay the right cords over the loop, under the bottom and over the top of the first cords.

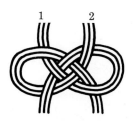

Continue by bringing the right cords under the first cords, over itself and under the first cords.

To even up the knot, pull the cords one at a time.

CHINESE CROWN

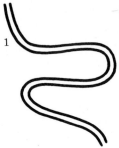

CHINESE CROWN: Place one cord on a board and curve it as shown above.

Weave cord 2 in and out of the curves formed by cord 1 as shown above. Pull cord ends tight.

ALTERNATING CHINESE CROWN: See instructions above for Chinese Crown and tie 3 in one row and 2 in the next. Continue this alternating pattern.

Double strand Chinese Crown

MONKEY'S FIST

1. MONKEY'S FIST: Make several winds around fingers, ending with a wind over one finger.

2. Wind cord horizontally around the first winds.

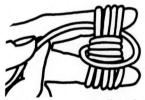

3. Continue by winding 3-4 times. Bring the cord thru the top loops.

4. After removing fingers, push a ½" diameter bead down in the center of the cords.

5. Bring the cord through the loops at the bottom.

6. Make several vertical winds. Pull the cords one at a time tightening each against the bead. See photo above.

The Guadalajara
Size, 10" x 9"

Instructions for knotting this bag
are available in the book **Macrame'
Designs**, published by Craft Course
Publishers.

Hints

WORKING BOARD: Lines drawn onto material covering a beaver, foam or cork board will help keep your projects shapely. The board at right can be purchased at most craft depts. and comes with the lines already drawn. The new macramé loom pictured was originally developed to aid the handicapped, but it's very helpful for anyone.

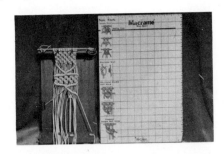

SPLICING: Cords may need to be spliced if extra length is needed or if the cord breaks. Unravel both ends to be joined, coat with white craft glue, twist ends together and allow glue to dry.

BUTTERFLY: To shorten long cords making them simpler to work with, start the butterfly about 8-10" from your project and tie around your fingers working down the cords. Put a rubberband in the middle.

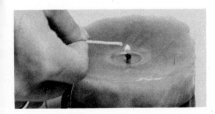

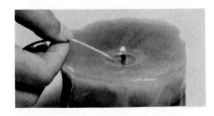

PREVENTION OF FRAYED ENDS: You can singe the ends of nylon or rayon cord with a candle.

For cotton or linen cords, dip the ends in wax or tie overhand knots on the ends.

APPROXIMATE CORD LENGTHS:
When working with projects with
fringed ends, cut the cords 4½ times
the desired length of the project.
When folding cords in half and tying
them on with Lark's heads, cut
cords 9-10 times the desired length
of the project.

WORKING HINTS: Mount work se-
curely on a board with pins. If it is
helpful, pin the knot-bearer to keep
it taut. Keep cords straight, avoid
twisting unless in the design.

DYEING CORDS: Soak and agitate
cord in soapy water to remove sizing
before dyeing. Rinse thoroughly
then dye cords to one shade darker
than desired color. Dyeing can be
done before or after knotting.

Glossary of Macramé Terms

KNOTTING CORDS (KNOTTERS)
are the cords which are used to tie
the knots.

FILLERS (ANCHOR CORDS) are
non-working cords, such as the center cords in the square knot.

A KNOT-BEARER is used in the
clove hitch patterns and knotters tie
around it. The angle the knot-bearer
is held in determines the direction of
the knots: horizontal, diagonal, or
vertical.

The HOLDING CORD is an object
onto which knotting cords are tied.
This can be another cord, belt buckle
rings, purse handle, dowels or sticks.
Cords can be attached with the Lark's
head or decorative picots may be
used.

SINNETS are "lengths of tied knots".

FLOATERS are unknotted cords.

Laguna Sawdust Festival, 1971
Photographed by Larry Cooper

Original macrame' by Jill Cooper
Curtain size 7ft. by 8ft.

CLASSIFIED INDEX